Snug as a Bug

Melanie McNeice

D&C

David and Charles

www.stitchcraftcreate.co.uk

Contents

Introduction

Welcome to a land of buggy delights where snails are multicoloured and the ladybugs dance amongst the flowers. When I first designed 'Snug as a Bug' – my new fabric collection for Riley Blake – I fell in love. The designs made me feel so happy and carefree – I simply adore this colourful world of cute bugs and pretty florals.

As soon as the fabric artwork was complete, I had project ideas buzzing around in my head. I just knew that I wanted to create a book of the same title to bring the characters and design motifs to life. How delighted I was when David & Charles were equally enthusiastic about my ideas, so giving me the opportunity to turn my imaginings into reality, and to share them all with you.

I hope that you find joy and delight in making these creations and that they will bring a sparkle to the eyes of the little loved ones you create them for.

Melly

www.mellyandme.com

Flower Garden Quilt

Wrap your precious little one in this gorgeous quilt to keep her as snug as a bug in a rug. Perfect to brighten up any room, this single bed sized quilt features simple piecing with some lovely appliqué blocks made using motifs from my 'Snug as a Bug' fabric collection. You can make more appliqué blocks, or mix and match the appliqué shapes in any way you choose, to create your own one-of-a-kind Flower Garden Quilt.

You will need

- 46cm (18in) yellow shade fabric
- 46cm (18in) pink shade fabric
- 30cm (12in) blue shade fabric
- 46cm (18in) each of a selection of 10 'Snug as a Bug' fabrics
- 46cm (18in) pink binding fabric
- 2.2m (2½yd) good-quality quilt wadding (batting)
- 4.4m (5yd) of your chosen fabric for backing
- 1m (40in) fusible webbing
- Six-strand embroidery thread (floss): dark pink, blue and green

Note: Use 100% cotton patchwork fabrics 106cm–114cm (42in–44in) wide for this project.

Finished size: 1.4m (55in) wide x 1.9m (75in) long

Cutting your fabrics

Note: Keep your fabric leftovers to be used for the appliqué motifs.

From yellow shade fabric:
Cut two squares measuring 29cm x 29cm (11½in x 11½in).
Cut two rectangles measuring 15.5cm x 29cm (6in x 11½in).
Cut four squares measuring 15.5cm x 15.5cm (6in x 6in).

From pink shade fabric:
Cut one square measuring 29cm x 29cm (11½in x 11½in).
Cut three rectangles measuring 15.5cm x 29cm (6in x 11½in).
Cut four squares measuring 15.5cm x 15.5cm (6in x 6in).

From blue shade fabric:
Cut one square measuring 29cm x 29cm (11½in x 11½in).
Cut one rectangle measuring 15.5cm x 29cm (6in x 11½in).
Cut five squares measuring 15.5cm x 15.5cm (6in x 6in).

From five of the 'Snug as a Bug' fabrics:
Cut one square measuring 29cm x 29cm (11½in x 11½in).
Cut two rectangles measuring 15.5cm x 29cm (6in x 11½in).
Cut three squares measuring 15.5cm x 15.5cm (6in x 6in).

From the remaining five 'Snug as a Bug' fabrics:
Cut three rectangles measuring 15.5cm x 29cm (6in x 11½in).
Cut four squares measuring 15.5cm x 15.5cm (6in x 6in).

Making the quilt

Note: Use a 6mm (¼in) seam allowance throughout.

one Trace the Flower Garden Quilt appliqué templates (see Templates) onto fusible webbing following the cutting instructions provided. Note, each template is made of several parts that need to be cut individually to make up the appliqué block designs. Use the photographs of the quilt to guide you. Rough-cut the template shapes outside the traced lines.

two Choose fabrics from your leftover pieces for each of the component parts of your appliqué templates. Make sure there is adequate contrast for touching fabrics in the final layout (see quilt photographs and note that the appliqué blocks are made using your shade fabrics as backgrounds). Once you are happy with your choices, iron the fusible webbing shapes to the wrong side of your selected fabric pieces. Cut out all the shapes along the traced lines on the fusible webbing.

three Working on one appliqué block at a time, peel the backing paper from the appliqué pieces and position them in the correct order onto the shade fabric of your choosing; iron to fuse all pieces in place. You should have four large square flower appliqué blocks (one of each design), four rectangle long, thin flower appliqué blocks (two of each design), five small square flower appliqué blocks, and three small square ladybug appliqué blocks.

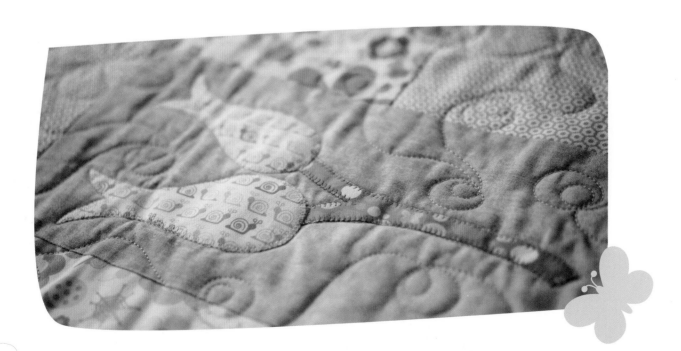

four Using either machine or hand blanket stitch (see Stitching Techniques), appliqué all pieces into place onto each of your blocks. To complete the ladybug blocks, mark the stitching lines for the antennae and work these in backstitch (see Stitching Techniques) using three strands of embroidery thread (floss).

five Take two squares measuring 15.5cm x 15.5cm (6in x 6in) randomly chosen from your shade, 'Snug as a Bug' and appliquéd blocks, and place together with right sides facing. Sew together along one edge to create a rectangle (see Fig. 1). Make 24 rectangles in this way. Press well, pressing seams to one side.

Fig. 1

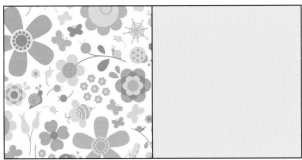

six Take two of the pieced rectangles and place together with right sides facing. Sew together along one long edge, ensuring that the centre seams meet, to create a pieced square. This is your 'A block' (see Fig. 2). Make a total of 12 'A blocks'. Press well, pressing seams to one side, and set aside.

Tip: Make sure the same fabrics do not meet in any of your quilt piecing. Try to have different colours and scales of print alongside each other for best results.

Fig. 2

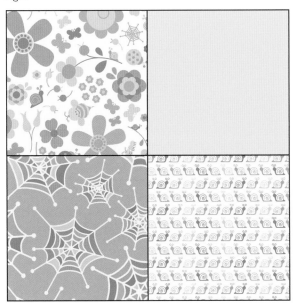

seven Take two rectangles measuring 15.5cm x 29cm (6in x 11½in) randomly chosen from your shade, 'Snug as a Bug' and appliquéd blocks, and place together with right sides facing. Sew together along one long edge to create a square (see Fig. 3). This is your 'B block' (see Fig. 3). Make a total of 14 'B blocks'. Press well, pressing seams to one side.

Fig. 3

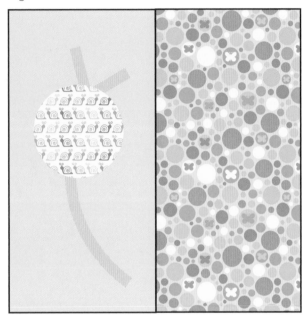

eight Take three of the A blocks and two of the B blocks. Positioning the B block rectangles vertically, sew the A blocks and B blocks together alternately, to create Row 1 of your quilt. Repeat to create Rows 3, 5 and 7, referring to the overhead photograph of the quilt.

nine Take three of the 29cm x 29cm (11½in x 11½in) fabric squares and two of the B blocks. Positioning the B block rectangles horizontally, sew the blocks together alternately to create Row 2 of your quilt. Repeat to create Rows 4 and 6, referring to the overhead photograph of the quilt.

ten Lay your pieced rows out in order on the floor and, once you are happy with the arrangement, sew the seven rows together along the length. To ensure that all seams and blocks meet evenly, you may like to pin your rows together before sewing (I recommend pinning and adding one row at a time). Once the stitching of the rows is completed, press seams to one side.

eleven To make a backing for your quilt, cut two lengths of backing fabric, each measuring 2.2m (87in) in length by the full width. Sew together along the 2.2m (87in) edge and press to one side. Your backing will be wider than required so trim the width only of your quilt backing to measure approximately 1.65m (65in).

Tip: For a quicker and more economical way to back your quilt, purchase 2.2m (87in) of wide quilt-backing fabric.

Row 1

Row 2

Row 3

Row 4

Row 5

Row 6

Row 7

twelve Make your quilt sandwich: place the backing right side facing down on a flat surface. Pull taut and tape the fabric down to your surface to avoid movement. In the same way, lay the wadding (batting) on top, and finally the pieced quilt top, right side facing up. Tack (baste) the layers together using curved basting pins, or by taking large tacking (basting) stitches through all layers at regular intervals.

thirteen Quilt as desired. I chose a custom quilting design with my longarm quilter but you could just as easily hand quilt or machine quilt using the stitch-in-the-ditch method. Avoid quilting within the appliqué motifs. It is much more effective to quilt an outline around the outside of the shapes to make them really pop out. Once your quilt is fully quilted, trim the wadding (batting) and backing edges to 6mm (1⁄4in) outside of your quilt top edges.

fourteen Cut seven lengths of your chosen binding fabric each measuring 6.5cm (2½in) by the full fabric width. Take your first two binding strips and place the trimmed ends on top of each other as shown in Fig. 4, and sew together at a 45-degree angle. Repeat with all strips to create one long length of binding. Trim the seam allowance and press all seams open. Fold the binding strip in half, wrong sides facing, all the way along its length and press well.

Fig. 4

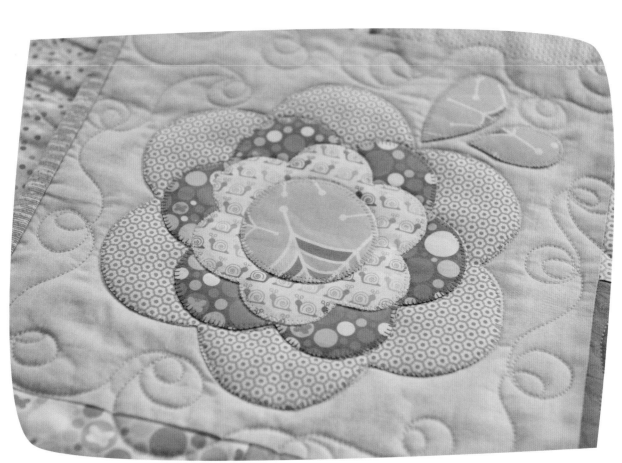

fifteen Starting 13cm (5in) from the beginning of your binding strip, start sewing the raw edge of your folded binding to the raw edge of your quilt front (Fig. 5).

Fig. 5

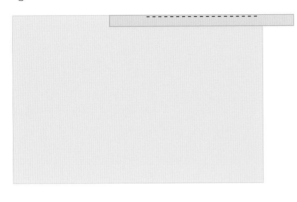

seventeen Continue to sew your binding in place all the way around the quilt, and finish and secure when you are approximately 25cm (10in) from your starting point. Laying the start and the end of your binding strips in place along the remaining quilt edge, trim the ends of your binding strip so that they overlap by 1.3cm (½in). Open the ends out and sew together, right sides facing. Refold the binding strip and sew the remaining section in place.

eighteen Fold the binding over the raw edges to the back of your quilt, enclosing the wadding (batting). Pin or clip in place. Working by hand, ladder stitch the neat folded edge of the binding to the quilt back, mitring the corners as you go.

Tip: When hand stitching your binding in place, make sure you use a thread colour that matches the binding fabric to make your stitches as invisible as possible.

sixteen When you reach a corner, stop and secure your stitching 6mm (¼in) from the corner edge (Fig. 6a). Fold your binding strip up and away from your quilt to create a 45-degree angle (Fig. 6b). Holding this fold in place, now fold the binding strip back down to lay neatly against the next edge of your quilt. Continue sewing your binding in place, beginning 6mm (¼in) from the corner (Fig. 6c).

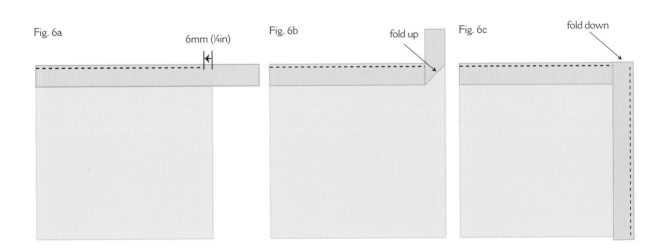

Fig. 6a   6mm (¼in)

Fig. 6b   fold up

Fig. 6c   fold down

Little Ladybug Bag

Every little girl loves carrying around her own special handbag 'just like mummy'. Knowing just how much my little girl adores ladybugs, I had the thought that it would be perfect to combine the two. The Little Ladybug Bag I have designed is the perfect size for carrying all that the little lady in your life needs to go about her busy day. Lift the ladybug's wings to reveal the secret pockets.

You will need

- 25.5cm (10in) x the full width of blue small floral print (front pocket, handles)
- 53cm x 65cm (21in x 26in) pink small floral print (main bag, lining)
- 10cm (4in) x the full width of white snail print (bag top)
- 50cm x 30cm (20in x 12in) raspberry spot fabric (wings)
- 38cm (15in) lightweight fusible fleece
- 110cm (44in) of 1.8cm (¾in) yellow bias tape

Finished size: 38cm (15in) high x 30cm (12in) wide

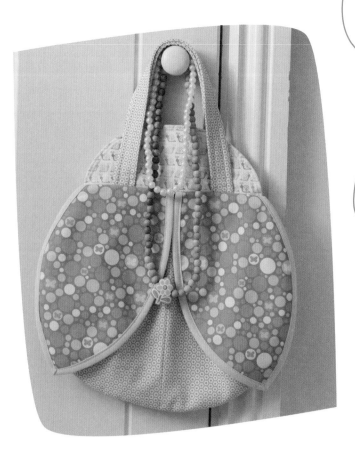

Cutting your fabrics

Note: Trace the Little Ladybug Bag templates (see Templates) onto template plastic, transferring all the markings, and carefully cut them out around the traced lines, following the instructions marked on the templates to make the full pocket and full main bag templates.

From the blue small floral print:
Draw around the pocket template once onto folded fabric (right sides together) and cut out along the drawn line to give you two pocket pieces.
Cut four strips measuring 4cm x 38cm (1½in x 15in) for the handles.

From the pink small floral print:
Draw around the main bag template twice onto folded fabric (right sides together) and cut out along the drawn lines to give you two main bag pieces and two lining pieces.

From the white snail print:
Draw around the bag top template twice onto folded fabric (right sides together) and cut out along the drawn lines to give you four bag top pieces.

From the raspberry spot print:
Draw around the wing template twice onto folded fabric (right sides together) and cut out along the drawn lines to give you four wing pieces.

From the lightweight fusible fleece:
Draw around the pocket template once, the main bag template twice, the bag top template twice, and the wing template twice (flipping the wing template for the second wing), and cut out along the drawn lines.
Cut two strips measuring 4cm x 38cm (1½in x 15in) for the handles.

Making the bag

Note: Use a 6mm (¼in) seam allowance throughout.

one Iron lightweight fusible fleece to the wrong side of the corresponding fabric pieces.

two Take the two pocket pieces and, working on one at a time, sew the pleats into place by folding the raw pleat edges on top of each other, right sides facing, and sewing into place.

three Place the pocket pieces together, right sides facing and sew along the top edge only. Turn right sides out and press. Topstitch the sewn edge with two lines of stitching. Tack (baste) the remaining raw edges of the pocket together evenly.

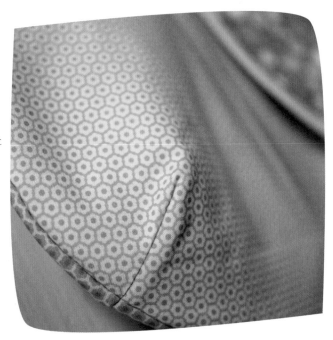

Tip: A single or double line of topstitching gives a neat, professional finish to bag seams and handles.

four Take the two main bag and two lining pieces and sew the pleats into place as in step 2.

five Take the main bag front (with fleece) and place the pocket on top right sides facing up. Ensure that the bottom edge and pleats meet and then machine tack (baste) the raw edges of the pocket evenly into place. Topstitch a line of stitching from the centre top to the centre bottom of the pocket, to create a double pocket (see Fig. 1).

Fig. 1

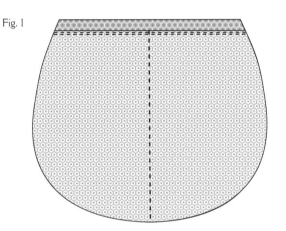

six Take the main bag front (with pocket) and the main bag back (with fleece) and place together with right sides facing. Sew together along the side and bottom edges, leaving the top edge open. Turn right side out.

seven Place the bag lining pieces together with right sides facing, and, leaving the top edge unstitched, sew together along the side and bottom edges, leaving a 10cm (4in) gap in the bottom edge for turning. **Do not** turn through at this stage.

eight Take one of the wing pieces with fleece and one without fleece and place together with wrong sides facing. Tack (baste) together all around the edges. Repeat to make the second wing.

nine Take a 56cm (22in) length of bias tape and fold in half along its length with wrong sides facing. Press very well. Bind the raw edge of the sides of the wing (**do not** bind the top straight edge): place the raw edge of the wing into the fold of the bias tape; make sure you catch both sides of the bias tape as you topstitch it in place around the edge, mitring the bottom corner as you go. Repeat for the second wing.

Tip: You can divide one or both pockets further by adding more lines of topstitching, to make, for example, a row of pencil pockets.

ten With the main bag right side up, position the wings, also right side up, onto the bag front so that they become flaps to cover the pockets. Tack (baste) the top raw edge of the wings to the top edge of the main bag front (see Fig. 2).

thirteen Take one of the bag top pieces with fleece and one without fleece and place together with right sides facing. Sew along the top curved edge only; turn and press. Topstitch with two lines of stitching. Repeat to make a second bag top.

Fig. 2

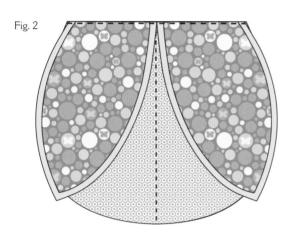

eleven Take one of the handle strips with fleece and one without fleece and place together with right sides facing. Sew along both long edges, turn and press. Topstitch a line of stitching along both sides of the handle strip. Repeat to make a second handle.

twelve With the main bag right side up, position one handle onto the bag front. Tack (baste) the raw ends of the handle to the top edge of the main bag front approx 4cm (1½in) from each side (see Fig. 3). Turn the bag over and repeat to attach the second handle to the bag back.

Fig. 3

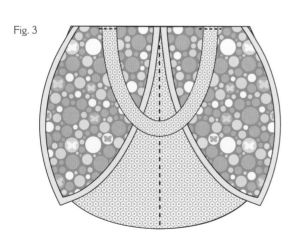

Tip: For a more secure bag opening, insert a magnetic closure into the lining of the bag top (on both sides) before attaching it to the main bag.

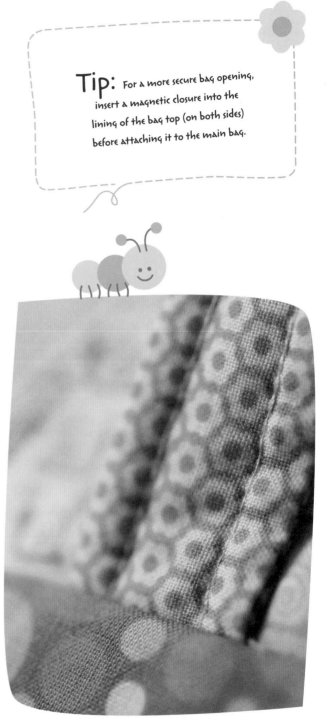

fourteen With the main bag right side up, position one bag top onto the bag front. Tack (baste) the raw ends of the bag top to the top edge of the main bag (see Fig. 4). Turn the bag over and repeat to attach the second bag top to the bag back.

fifteen Place the main bag (right side facing out) into the inside-out lining bag. Make sure that all the layers are lying flat and straight between the two bag layers and that the top edges are aligning, then tack (baste) into place. Sew the bag top together securely.

sixteen Turn the bag right side out through the gap in the bottom edge of the lining. Fold the lining inside the bag and press the top edge well.

seventeen Fold the wings up so that they are out of the way, then topstitch all the way around the top edge of the main bag. Slipstitch the gap in the lining closed.

Fig. 4

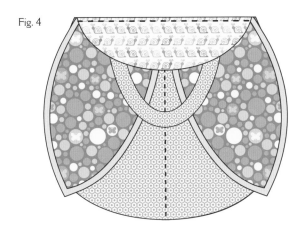

Sebastian the Snail

Sebastian the Snail is such a sweet little creature. He goes about his day as silent as can be, crawling amongst the beautiful flowers in the garden, and he would make the perfect companion for any little explorer. At the end of the day, he likes nothing better than coming indoors, cuddled tightly in little arms.

You will need

- One fat quarter large floral print (main body)

- 30cm x 46cm (12in x 18in) small floral print (shell, antennae)

- 30cm x 20cm (12in x 8in) lightweight fusible fleece

- Small scraps of blue and white wool felt (eyes)

- Six-strand embroidery thread (floss): blue, dark grey and pink

- Good-quality polyester toy filling

- Good-quality polyester thread

Finished size: 19cm (7½in) high x 22cm (8½in) long

Making the softie

Note: Use a 6mm (¼in) seam allowance throughout, using a very small stitch on your sewing machine.

ONE Trace the Sebastian the Snail templates (see Templates) onto template plastic, transferring all the markings, and carefully cut them out around the traced lines.

two Fold the main body fabric in half with right sides together. Draw around the main body template once onto the folded fabric and cut out along the drawn line. Unfold the fabric and draw around the head and base gusset templates once onto the wrong side of the single layer of fabric. Cut out along the drawn lines.

three Take the head and base gusset pieces and machine stitch together along the neckline edge as marked, with right sides facing.

four Take one of the main body pieces and the joined gusset piece. Matching up the neckline seam of the gusset with the neck on the snail's main body, tack (baste) the gusset in place with right sides facing, working from the snail's tail, along the base and all the way around the head. Machine stitch the gusset in place.

eight Mark the shell spiral onto one shell front piece and one shell back piece. Interface one shell gusset piece and the two shell pieces marked with the spirals with lightweight fusible fleece. Hand stitch the spirals with two strands of pink embroidery thread (floss) using small chain stitches (see Stitching Techniques).

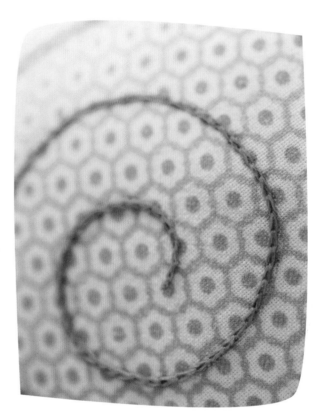

five Tack (baste) the remaining raw edge of the gusset to the second main body piece with right sides facing. Machine stitch in place and then continue to sew the remaining raw edges of the snail's back together, leaving the turning gap open as indicated.

six Carefully snip the tail point and the corners. Turn Sebastian right side out, and stuff firmly with toy filling. Ladder stitch the turning gap closed (see Stitching Techniques).

seven Fold the shell fabric in half with right sides facing. Draw around the shell template twice and the shell gusset template once onto folded fabric and cut out along the drawn lines.

nine Tack (baste) the gusset (with fleece) in place between the two hand embroidered shell pieces with right sides together, taking care to match the stars marked on your shell and gusset templates. Once evenly tacked (basted), machine stitch in place. Repeat with the remaining shell and gusset pieces (without fleece) to make the shell lining.

ten Place the main shell and shell lining pieces together with right sides facing, and machine stitch all the way around the raw edges. Snip into the corners and curves. Cut a turning gap in the centre of the shell lining, making sure that you cut the lining layer only, and turn the shell right side out through this gap. Press, then topstitch all the way around the bottom edge.

eleven Stuff the shell lightly and then sit this on the snail's back in the desired position. Pin or tack (baste) into place. Ladder stitch the inner bottom edge of the shell onto the snail's back using a double strand of strong polyester thread (see Stitching Techniques). When you are approx 2.5cm–5cm (1in– 2in) from finishing the sewing, stuff the shell firmly through the remaining gap until you are happy with the shape. Ladder stitch the gap closed.

Tip: If the snail is well stuffed, you will find it is much easier to stitch the face details and attach the antennae.

twelve Take the remaining shell fabric and fold in half, right sides together. Draw the antennae templates onto the folded fabric but **do not** cut out.

thirteen Machine stitch the antennae along the drawn lines, leaving the bottom straight edges open for turning. Cut the antennae out approx 3mm–6mm (⅛in–¼in) outside the sewn lines. Turn right side out and stuff with toy filling, taking care not to damage the seams. To turn small pieces easily, insert a pair of tweezers into your unturned piece, grab the end and pull it through the opening. When stuffing small and fiddly pieces, it can be helpful to use the blunt end of a wooden skewer to push in small pieces of stuffing one at a time. Always work slowly and patiently to ensure that you do not split the seams. Fold the raw edges to the inside, then stitch the antennae in place on the snail's head by ladder stitching along the folded bottom edge (see Stitching Techniques). Sew around the base of each antenna twice to make sure they are securely stitched on.

fourteen Draw around the pupil template twice onto white wool felt and cut out along the drawn lines. Position the pupils onto blue wool felt, making sure there is adequate space around each one. To appliqué the pupils in place, blanket stitch by hand or machine (see Stitching Techniques). Mark the eye dot inside each pupil and work a French knot with six strands of grey embroidery thread (floss). Draw the eye template around each pupil and cut out the completed eyes along the drawn lines.

fifteen Position the eyes onto the snail's face and glue tack (baste) into position. Using two strands of blue embroidery thread (floss), blanket stitch the eyes to secure in place. Mark the stitching line for the snail's mouth between the eyes, and sew with chain stitch using two strands of dark grey embroidery thread (floss) (see Stitching Techniques).

Tip: You could scale the templates down by varying degrees on a photocopier, to create a whole family of snails.

Flutter-by Mobile

Butterflies are so peaceful, so beautiful, and bring wonder to all. A butterfly mobile, hanging above the cot, is the perfect way to capture the imagination of a newborn baby. Little ones will be enthralled, watching these dancing butterflies flutter-by, as they settle into a sweet sleep. You could make up more little butterflies as the perfect take-along toys for babies on the go.

You will need

- 25.5cm x 25.5cm (10in x 10in) each of a selection of six 'Snug as a Bug' fabrics
- 2m (2⅛yd) of 1.8cm (¾in) wide bias tape to match your fabrics
- 10cm (4in) lightweight fusible fleece
- One 20cm (8in) wooden embroidery hoop
- Wooden beads: one 40mm and one 25mm
- Small scraps of fabric to cover beads
- 1m (40in) fine 2mm aqua cord (antennae)
- Approx 4m (4⅜yd) fine white 2mm cord (hanging strings)
- Fabric glue
- Black six-strand embroidery thread (floss)
- Good-quality polyester thread
- Good-quality polyester toy filling
- Use of a drill
- Large-eyed dollmaker's needle

Finished size: 50cm (20in) high x 20cm (8in) wide

Making the mobile

Note: Use a 6mm (¼in) seam allowance throughout, using a very small stitch on your sewing machine.

one Trace the Flutter-by Mobile templates (see Templates) onto template plastic, transferring all the markings, and cut them out around the traced lines.

two Take one of the pieces of fabric measuring 25.5cm x 25.5cm (10in x 10in) and cut into two pieces measuring 25.5cm x 15.5cm (10in x 6in) and 25.5cm x 10cm (10in x 4in). Set aside the smaller piece of fabric for now.

Tip: When choosing fabrics, use fun contrasting colours to make the mobile really eye catching.

three Take the 25.5cm x 15.5cm (10in x 6in) piece of fabric and fold in half with right sides facing. Draw around the butterfly body template onto the folded fabric, but **do not** cut out. Machine stitch the body around the drawn line, leaving the antennae gaps open as indicated. Cut out the butterfly body approx 6mm (¼in) outside the sewn line and snip corners.

four Measure two 7.5cm (3in) lengths of aqua cord and, to keep it from unravelling, secure at either end with a little tape before cutting. Insert the cords into the antennae gaps, so that all but the very ends of the cords sit within the head. Sew the ends of the cord in place securely.

five Snip a small slit as marked on the template on one side only of the butterfly, then turn right side out through this gap (note, the turning gap will be hidden by the wings later). Stuff the butterfly firmly with polyester toy filling.

six Tie a knot in the ends of the antennae, then trim to the desired length. Mark the eyes and mouth onto the front of the butterfly (note, the back of the butterfly is the side with the turning gap). Working with two strands of black embroidery thread (floss), stitch the eyes with satin stitch and the mouth with chain stitch (see Stitching Techniques).

seven Measure a 1m (40in) length of white cord and secure at either end with a little tape before cutting to prevent it from unravelling; tie a knot at one end and thread the unknotted end in the dollmaker's needle. Take the threaded needle from the inside of the butterfly (access through the turning gap in the back of the butterfly) and come out on the back of the butterfly's head marked with an 'X' on the template. The knot should catch inside the butterfly's head to give you a long hanging cord (see Fig. 1). Slipstitch the turning gap closed.

Fig. 1

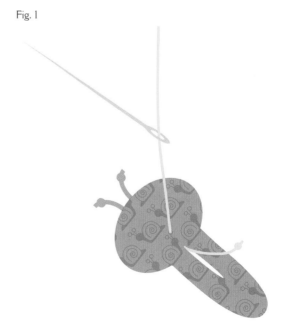

eight Repeat steps 2–7 to make five more butterfly bodies, but in step 7 use a 50cm (20in) length of white cord.

nine Take the set-aside piece of fabric measuring 25.5cm x 10cm (10in x 4in) and iron a piece of fusible fleece measuring 13cm x 10cm (5in x 4in) to the wrong side of half of this. Fold the fabric in half with right sides facing, and draw around the wing template onto the fleece side; **do not** cut out. Machine stitch the wings all the way around the drawn line.

ten Cut out the wings approx 3mm (⅛in) outside the sewn line, and snip the corners. Snip a small slit (see template) on one side only of the wings, then turn right side out through this gap. Press well, then topstitch all the way around the edges.

eleven Repeat steps 9 and 10 to make five more sets of butterfly wings.

twelve Take one of the butterfly body pieces and one of the butterfly wings. Work a line of medium-sized running stitches (see Stitching Techniques) in the centre of the back of the wings, from top to bottom, alongside the turning gap, and gather slightly. Now ladder stitch the centre line of the wings onto the back of the butterfly (see Stitching Techniques), covering both turning gaps in the process. Go over the stitching twice to make sure the wings are securely fastened.

thirteen Take the 20cm (8in) embroidery hoop; separate the rings and put aside the screw mechanism ring as this is not required for this project. Evenly mark the ring into sixths. Working with a drill fitted with a 2mm–3mm drill bit, drill a hole into the ring at each marked interval (see Fig. 2).

Fig. 2

fourteen To cover the ring with fabric, use fabric glue to fix the end of the 2m (2⅛yd) length of bias tape on the inside of the ring, then wind the tape around the ring fixing it in place with glue as you go. When you cover a drilled hole, make sure glue does not go inside the hole, and mark the position of the hole with a small dot for easy reference later. Make sure to finish on the inside of the ring and secure the end well. Set-aside the unused bias tape (note, you will need a small piece at least 2.5cm/1in long in step 21), and allow to dry completely.

fifteen Take one of the butterflies and thread the loose end of its cord into the dollmaker's needle. Thread the cord through one of the holes in the ring working from the outside to the inside of the ring. Repeat to string all of the butterflies through the ring.

sixteen When all the butterflies have been strung through the ring, adjust the ends of the cords until they are all even, intersecting at the desired length where the bead will be threaded on to hide the cord ends. (Note, the longer cord will become the hanging cord for the mobile.)

Tip: Make sure that your large bead has a generous enough hole to allow the cord intersection to fit inside it.

seventeen Where the cords intersect, secure them together with a tied piece of thread, then machine stitch over the intersection several times to ensure a strong join. Trim back the shorter cord ends, leaving the longer one in place.

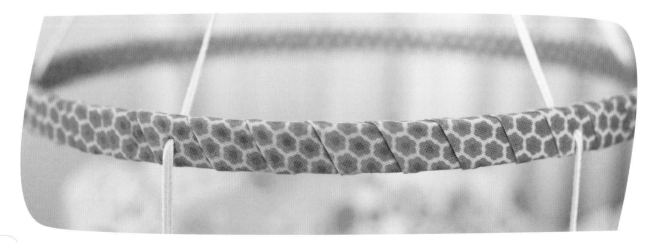

eighteen To cover your beads with fabric you first need to cut a small strip of fabric that is approx 1.3cm (½in) longer that the circumference of your bead by half this length. Snip into the top and bottom edges of your fabric strip about every 6mm (¼in) as shown in Fig. 3.

Fig. 3

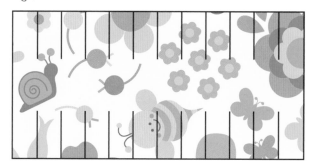

nineteen Coat the middle unsnipped section of the wrong side of your fabric strip with glue. Wrap the glued fabric strip around the circumference of your bead ensuring it lays neatly and smoothly, and that the overlapped sections are well secured with glue. Working on the top edge of your bead first, and gluing one fringe piece at a time, secure each fringe piece straight up over the top edge of the bead, pushing the end neatly into the bead hole using a knitting needle or other round-ended tool. Repeat for the bottom edge of the bead. Allow your bead to dry completely before using.

twenty Once the beads have completely dried, thread the cord first through the large bead, then through the small bead. Slide the beads down to cover the meeting point of the cords; secure the beads in place with glue if you choose to.

twenty-one You may need to trim the long cord to give you the desired length for hanging the mobile. Fold the end of the cord onto itself by approx 2.5cm (1in) and secure well before trimming the end. Take a small piece of the remaining bias tape and wrap this around the join, folding under the end to neaten, and sew in place. The finished mobile is ready to be hung.

Tip: As an alternative to covering with fabric, the ring and beads could be painted. Sand before painting and allow them to dry really well before continuing.

Bug in a Rug

I will always remember how attached my little one was to her 'blanky' when she was a baby. By combining a cute toy with a soft and snuggly blanket, my Bug in a Rug is the perfect comforter for your child. For a gorgeous themed nursery, the sweet and cuddly Bug in a Rug has been made in colours to match the Flower Garden Quilt.

You will need

- 53cm x 53cm (21in x 21in) pink soft blanket fabric
- One fat quarter yellow web patterned fabric (binding, head)
- 15.5cm x 35.5cm (6in x 14in) aqua spot fabric (wings, antennae)
- 10cm x 10cm (4in x 4in) pink shade fabric (face)
- 15.5cm x 10cm (6in x 4in) lightweight fusible fleece
- 10cm x 10cm (4in x 4in) fusible webbing
- Six-strand embroidery thread (floss): pink and turquoise
- Good-quality polyester toy filling
- Good-quality polyester thread in a colour to match your blanket fabric

Finished size: 50cm (20in) square

Making the snuggle blanket

Note: Use a 6mm (¼in) seam allowance throughout.

one Trace the Bug in a Rug templates (see Templates) onto template plastic, transferring all the markings, and cut them out around the traced lines.

two Cut your soft blanket fabric into a neat even square measuring 50cm x 50cm (20in x 20in).

three First prepare the binding strips for edging the blanket fabric. Cut four strips measuring 6.5cm x 52cm (2½in x 20½in) from your fat quarter of patterned fabric.

Tip: I have chosen minky for my soft blanket fabric, which is a very soft fabric that feels like plush velour. Softer than fleece, it has a short 'fur' pile and is extremely cuddly.

four Take one of the binding strips and place it on an ironing board, right side facing down. Fold in the short ends by 6mm (¼in) and press in place; now fold in the long raw edges by 6mm (¼in) and press in place (see Fig. 1). Fold the whole strip in half along the length with wrong sides facing, and press. Repeat to make three more binding strips.

Tip: If you prefer you could use satin ribbon to bind the blanket.

Fig. 1

five Take one prepared (folded) binding strip and place it over one side edge of the soft blanket fabric square. Tack (baste) or pin into place ensuring that the strip is evenly positioned over both sides of the blanket fabric and that the ends meet the corners of the fabric square. Topstitch the inside edge of the binding strip onto the blanket, making sure that the stitching is securing both sides of the fabric as you go. Repeat to attach a binding strip on the opposite side of the blanket square.

six Take a third binding strip, open the main fold, and place the strip on the ironing board, right side facing down. Now fold in the corners to create triangles (see Fig. 2). Press well, then fold the strip in half along the length once again. Press well once more.

Tip: If you are using minky or another stretch fabric, take care not to stretch the fabric as you sew or the blanket may be distorted out of shape.

Fig. 2

seven Fit the prepared binding strip over the edge of one of the unbound sides of the blanket so that the points of the triangle meet the corners of the blanket. Tack (baste) or pin in place, then topstitch the inside edge of the binding strip, and into the corner angles (see Fig. 3), to secure in place. Repeat to attach the final binding strip on the opposite side. Put the blanket aside.

Fig. 3

eight Take the remainder of the fat quarter fabric and fold in half with right sides facing. Draw the head template twice onto the folded fabric and cut out along the drawn lines, to give you four head pieces. Transfer the pleat markings to the wrong side of the head pieces.

nine Using a small machine stitch, sew the pleats in place on the wrong side of the head pieces and trim excess fabric.

ten Place two of the head pieces together, with right sides facing, so that the pleats and edges meet. Again using a small stitch, sew together along the centre front seam. Repeat for the remaining two head pieces. You now have a head front and a head back.

eleven Place the head front and head back together with right sides facing, and sew together along the side and top edges only, leaving the antennae gaps open as indicated. The straight neckline edge at the bottom remains open but **do not** turn through yet.

twelve Take the wing/antennae patterned fabric and cut a piece from it measuring 15.5cm x 15.5cm (6in x 6in). Fold in half with right sides facing. Draw around the antenna template twice onto the folded fabric, making sure to leave plenty of space in between. Machine stitch around the drawn lines of the antennae leaving the bottom straight ends open as indicated on the template. Cut each antenna out by cutting approx 3mm–6mm (⅛in–¼in) outside the sewn line. Turn the antennae right side out, then stuff firmly with small pieces of the polyester toy filling. When fully stuffed, tack (baste) the raw ends closed.

thirteen Insert the antennae into the gaps at the top of the head, so that the raw tacked (basted) edges of the antennae meet the top edge of the gaps and the antennae curve outwards; sew the gaps closed, following the curve of the head, to secure the antennae in place. Now turn the head right side out.

fourteen Take the remaining wing/antennae patterned fabric and iron the piece of lightweight fusible fleece measuring 15.5cm x 10cm (6in x 4in) to the wrong side of half of this. Fold the fabric in half with right sides facing, and draw around the wing template twice onto the fleece side of the folded fabric, leaving space in between. **Do not** cut out.

Tip: To make turning the thin antenna quick and easy, insert a pair of tweezers, grip the end and pull through.

fifteen Machine stitch the wings around the drawn lines, leaving the straight ends open as indicated. Cut out the wings approx 6mm (¼in) outside the sewn lines. Turn through and press well. Topstitch the wings approx 3mm (⅛in) in from the seam edge. Take one of the wings, fold the raw straight edge onto itself and tack (baste) in place (see Fig. 4) to give the wing its distinctive 'fluttering' shape. Repeat for the second wing.

Fig. 4

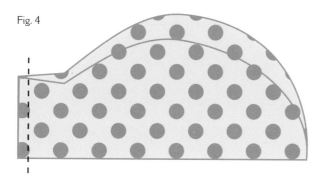

sixteen Take one of the wings and place it onto the side seam of the bug's head, making sure that the wing is facing forwards. It should be centred over the head's side seam, and the raw edges of the wing and head neckline should meet. Sew the wing onto the head along the fill line. Repeat on the other side with the remaining wing, again making sure that it is facing forwards.

seventeen Stuff the head firmly to the fill line with polyester toy filling; fold in the remaining raw edges of the head and wings and push inside the head.

eighteen Take the blanket and fold in half and half again to mark the centre point. Position the head at the centre mark on the right side of the blanket, and using a double thickness of strong polyester thread, ladder stitch the head in place (see Stitching Techniques). Make sure that the raw seams are enclosed within the head and that the stitching is roughly at the level of the fill line. Ladder stitch in a circle following the natural shape of the neckline, then go around again to attach the head securely.

nineteen Iron the fusible webbing to the wrong side of the pink shade (face) fabric. Draw around the face template onto the fusible webbing side and cut out along the drawn line. Peel off the paper backing and iron the face onto the front of the head. Using two strands of pink embroidery thread (floss), blanket stitch the face in place (see Stitching Techniques). Mark the eyes and mouth onto the face using a pencil, then stitch the face details using two strands of turquoise embroidery thread (floss), working the eyes with satin stitch and the mouth with backstitch (see Stitching Techniques).

Tip: If you are after a more compact comforter, you can reduce the fabric square to 30cm x 30cm (12in x 12in) and the binding strips to 32cm (12½in) in length.

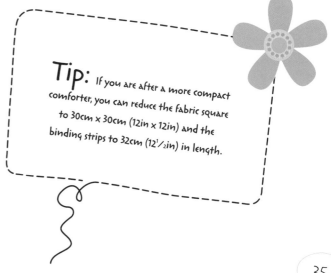

Stitching Techniques

Backstitch

Backstitch creates a continuous line of stitching so it's ideal for defining shapes.

Chain stitch

This stitch creates a nice thick decorative line.

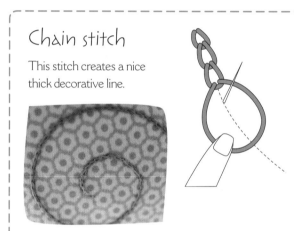

Blanket stitch

This edging stitch is used to secure appliquéd fabric pieces.

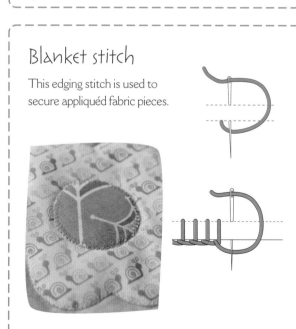

French knot

The double-wrap French knot creates a prominent raised dot, which is ideal for adding a centre to toy eye pupils.

Ladder stitch for closing gaps

This stitch is used to sew turning gaps closed and to attach the quilt binding securely.

Running stitch

A simple stitch used for decorative embroidery, or for gathering as on the Flutter-by Mobile butterfly wings.

Satin stitch

First backstitch around the outside edge of the shape and then satin stitch over the stitching.

Ladder stitch for attaching parts

Ladder stitch is also used to attach parts to soft toys. This method is usually used so that the attachment will either sit flat against or protrude from the stuffed toy. Follow the ladder stitch diagram for closing gaps, but make one stitch in the edge of the attachment, then make the next stitch in the body of the toy. The ladder stitches need to be sewn into the body following the shape of the attachment so that the latter retains its shape.

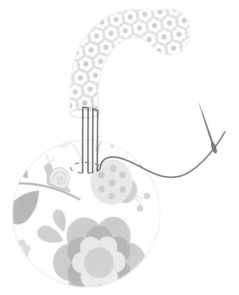

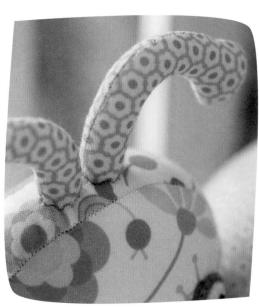

Templates

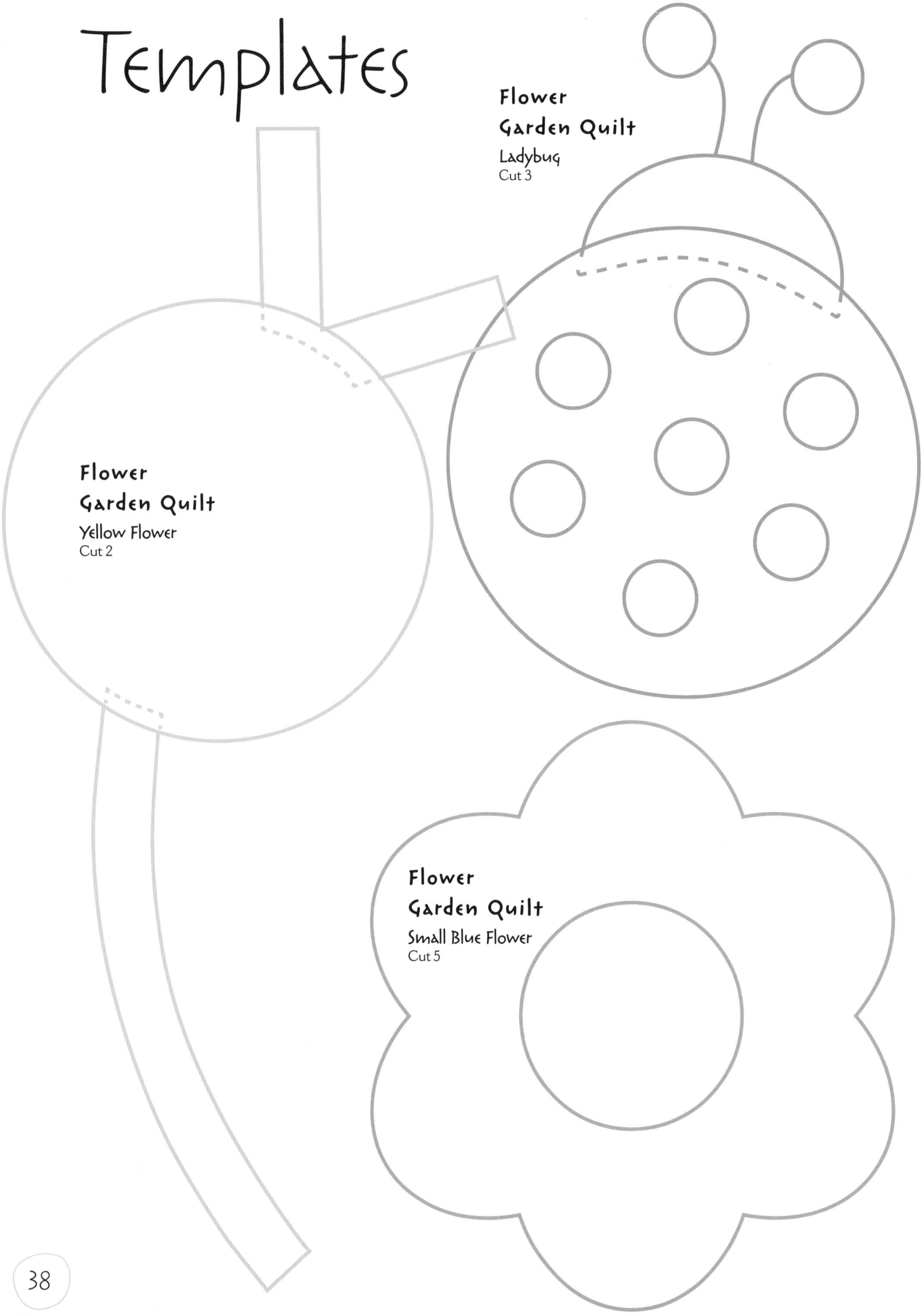

**Flower
Garden Quilt**

Ladybug
Cut 3

**Flower
Garden Quilt**

Yellow Flower
Cut 2

**Flower
Garden Quilt**

Small Blue Flower
Cut 5

Flower Garden Quilt
Large Pink Flower
Cut 1

cut 4 petals

Trace mirror image of the four flower pieces only

Flower Garden Quilt
Large Green Flower
Cut 1

Flower Garden Quilt
Large Blue Flower
Cut 1

cut 5 petals

cut 2 circles

39

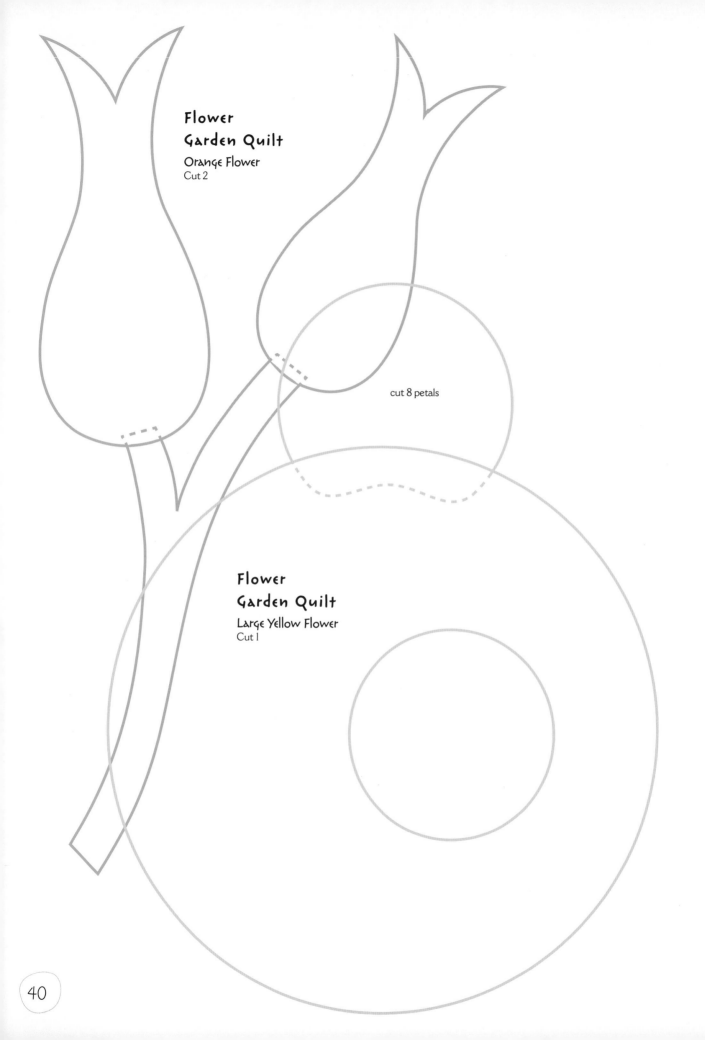

**Flower
Garden Quilt**

Orange Flower
Cut 2

cut 8 petals

**Flower
Garden Quilt**

Large Yellow Flower
Cut 1

40

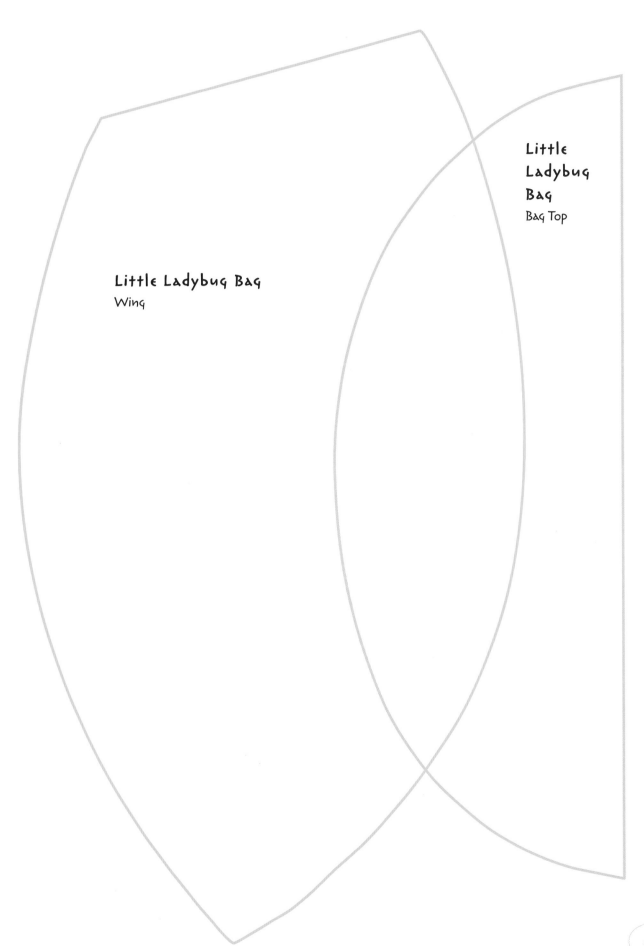

Little Ladybug Bag

Wing

**Little
Ladybug
Bag**
Bag Top

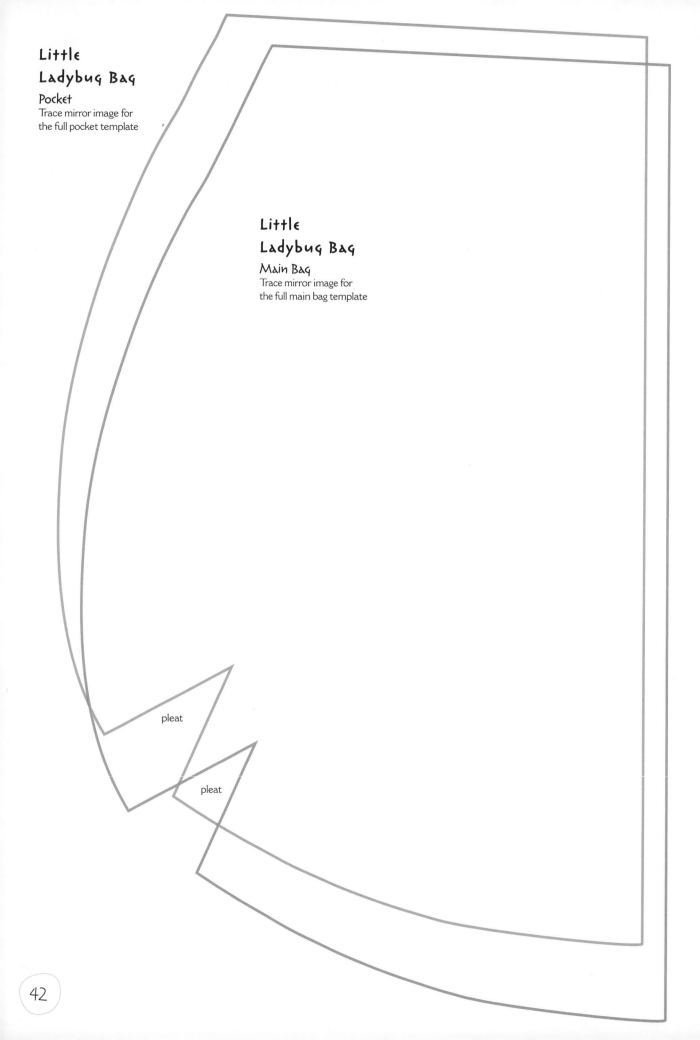

Little
Ladybug Bag
Pocket
Trace mirror image for
the full pocket template

Little
Ladybug Bag
Main Bag
Trace mirror image for
the full main bag template

pleat

pleat

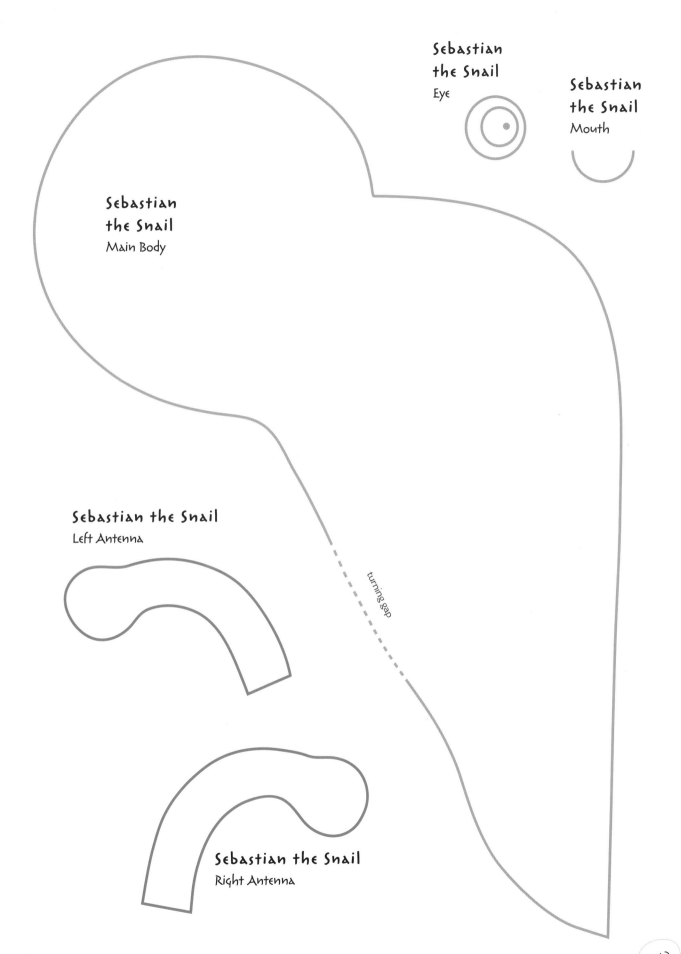

Sebastian
the Snail

Eye

Sebastian
the Snail

Mouth

Sebastian
the Snail

Main Body

Sebastian the Snail

Left Antenna

turning gap

Sebastian the Snail

Right Antenna

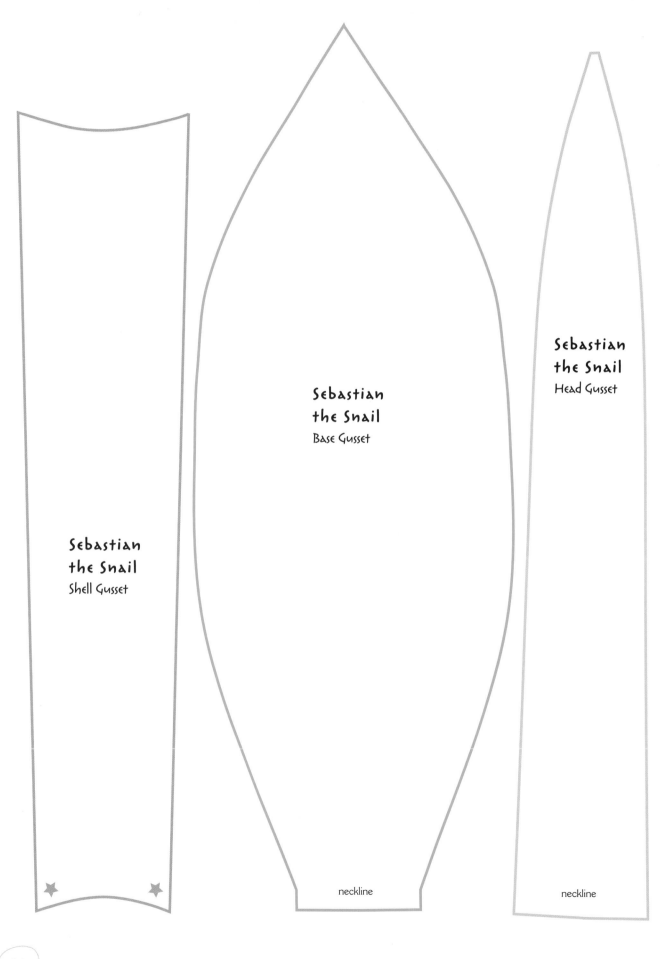

Sebastian the Snail

Shell Gusset

Sebastian the Snail

Base Gusset

neckline

Sebastian the Snail

Head Gusset

neckline

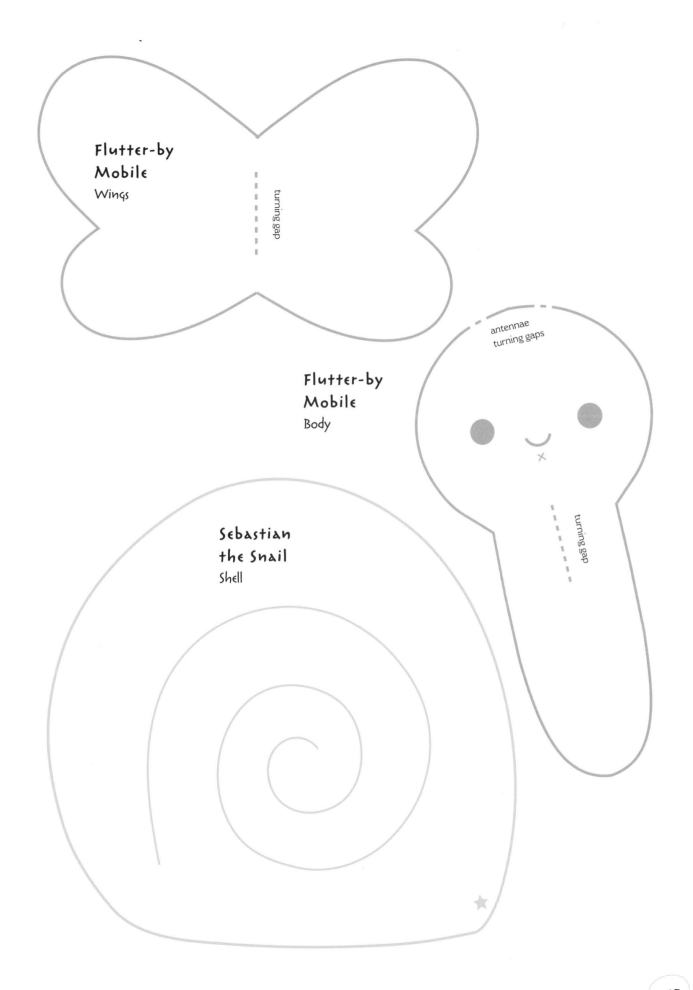

**Flutter-by
Mobile**
Wings

turning gap

**Flutter-by
Mobile**
Body

antennae
turning gaps

turning gap

**Sebastian
the Snail**
Shell

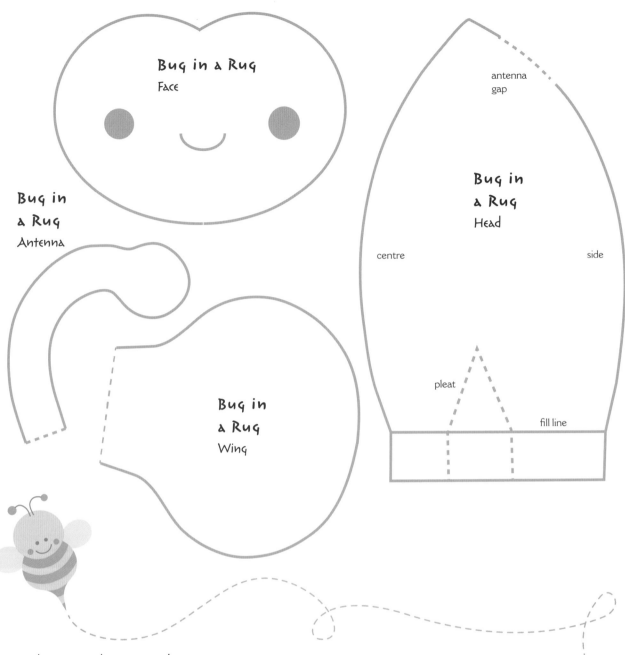

Bug in a Rug
Face

Bug in a Rug
Antenna

Bug in a Rug
Wing

Bug in a Rug
Head

antenna gap

centre

side

pleat

fill line

About the Author

Melanie McNeice is a pattern designer based in Melbourne, Australia. Melly's adventures in sewing began just nine years ago after she found herself a stay-at-home mum with the desire to still be productive. Her passion for sewing grew quickly after her sister encouraged her to give it a try, and only 12 months after beginning to sew, she tried her hand at design under the pattern label Melly & Me.

Melly aims to design items that are original and fun, achievable in a day, and useable in everyday life. To date she has created in excess of 90 contemporary sewing patterns, including bright, quirky toys and wearable purses, as well as fun, modern quilts. She has had two books of her work published, *Kaleidoscope* and *Sewn Toy Tales*, and she teaches across Australia. Melly recently began her journey in fabric design, and she has released three fabric collections since 2010. She takes inspiration from her two young children, childhood memories, the beauty of nature, and a love of fun and colour.

Acknowledgements

I would like to thank:

- Riley Blake for their partnership in bringing my new fabric collection 'Snug as a Bug' to life. It is an honour to work with such an amazing fabric company.
- Sue Daley from Mill House Collections for supplying Riley Blake fabrics for inclusion in this book.
- Anita Ellis from Hillside Quilting for the stunning custom quilting work she has done on the Flower Garden Quilt.
- The team at F&W Media International for their enthusiasm and support, and for making this book happen.
- All of my wonderful family, especially my sister Rosie and my parents for their continual support and for starting me on my design journey.
- But most importantly, I want to thank my truly amazing husband, Scott McNeice, without whom this book would never have gone from a thought process to a reality. Thank you for being my number one encourager, my unfailing support, my comedic relief, and for always believing in me 100%. I love you, my Scotty Dog!

Suppliers

Australia

Melly & Me
www.mellyandme.com
mellyandme@bigpond.com

Under the Mulberry Tree
www.underthemulberrytree.com

The Oz Material Girls
www.theozmaterialgirls.com

Fabric Patch
www.fabricpatch.com.au

Ballarat Patchwork
www.ballaratpatchwork.com.au

Patchwork with Gail B
www.patchworkwithgailb.com

Creative Abundance
www.creativeabundance.com.au

USA

Pink Chalk Fabrics
www.pinkchalkfabrics.com

Pine Needles
www.pineneedlesonline.com

Heartsong Quilts
www.heartsongquilts.com

UK

Hulu Crafts
www.hulacrafts.co.uk

Prints to Polka Dots
www.printstopolkadots.co.uk

Stitch Craft Create
www.stitchcraftcreate.co.uk

The Fat Quarters
www.thefatquarters.co.uk

Index

A DAVID & CHARLES BOOK

© F&W Media International, Ltd 2013

David & Charles is an imprint of F&W Media International, Ltd
Brunel House, Forde Close, Newton Abbot, TQ12 4PU, UK

F&W Media International, Ltd is a subsidiary of F+W Media, Inc
10151 Carver Road, Suite #200, Blue Ash, OH 45242, USA

Text and Designs © Melanie McNeice 2013
Layout and Photography © F&W Media International, Ltd 2013

First published in the UK and USA in 2013

Melanie McNeice has asserted her right to be identified as author of this work in accordance with the Copyright, Designs and Patents Act, 1988.

A catalogue record for this book is available from the British Library.

ISBN-13: 978-1-4463-0382-5 paperback
ISBN-10: 1-4463-0382-9 paperback

Printed in China by RR Donnelley for:
F&W Media International, Ltd
Brunel House, Forde Close, Newton Abbot, TQ12 4PU, UK

10 9 8 7 6 5 4 3 2 1

Craft Community Leader: Alison Myer
Editor: Jeni Hennah
Project Editor: Cheryl Brown
Junior Art Editor: Anna Fazakerley
Photographer: Jack Kirby
Production Manager: Beverley Richardson

F+W Media publishes high quality books on a wide range of subjects.
For more great book ideas visit: **www.stitchcraftcreate.co.uk**